THE WORLD IS YOURS

Turning Vision Into Reality

JEFF MOORE

authorHOUSE®

AuthorHouse™
1663 Liberty Drive, Suite 200
Bloomington, IN 47403
www.authorhouse.com
Phone: 1-800-839-8640

First published by AuthorHouse 3/4/2008

ISBN: 978-1-4343-6350-3 (sc)

*Printed in the United States of America
Bloomington, Indiana*

This book is printed on acid-free paper.

This book is dedicated to my rather large family that seems to grow every day. Here are a couple of shout-outs I just could not miss.

Big Ups to: Mom, Sarah, Wojtek, Kellogg, Brent, C-rad, Johnny, Palm 3, Jill, Bree, Mike D, Cat, Wizzy and Megs, Janelle, Hayes, Jenks, Heather, Ian, Tony, Lyssa, my whole Milestone's crew past and present, Stevie Hops, Janet and Jill, Kyla Kadlac and the entire school of Fred C. Cook, Carol, Barb, Cathy and Doug, Roy Zakka, all of Team Features, especially Jeff Bellamy, Matt Clulow, Julie Betts, Jess Taggs, Alexis Green and anyone else I may not have mentioned here (I'm trying to write a short book this time).

Dream Big, Live Bigger

I failed grade five! Can you believe that? I failed grade five! I always wondered why I couldn't have failed one of those respectable grades like kindergarten or grade one, but no, I had to fail grade five. In fact, to be honest, I don't remember passing much in school ever ... except gym. I passed gym just fine - in fact I graduated with 7 gym credits ...not bad!

So here's the dilly: I'm not coming at you like I am some moral authority on anything except my beliefs. Really I'm just some dude. Just some dude who holds onto the idea that you can do or be anything you want in life. I am not a law of attraction guy, meaning I don't think that all you have to do is stick out your hand and think happy thoughts for things to appear. In fact I don't believe in a lot of what most speakers and authors are out there saying today - too many preach at a level they don't live at. I don't know that there is any secret to success except learning the lessons of failure and as Nike put it so well ... JUST DO IT.

My hope for you, the reader is that this book provides you with some insight that you can take with you and help you to shape and create the life you deserve.

I have been through some rough times and lived some amazing times and want to remind you that life is good, especially when you actually live it, so go out there and get 'er done.

"Hope is not blind optimism. It's not ignoring the enormity of the tasks ahead or the roadblocks that stand in our path.

It's not sitting on the sidelines or shirking from a fight. Hope is that thing inside us that insists, despite all the evidence to the contrary, that something better awaits us if we have the courage to reach for it and to work for it and to fight for it"

-Barack Obama Iowa Caucus Victory Speech

CONTENTS

CHAPTER 1

Becoming Your Own Leader
Compound Interest and Giving Meaning

"You're the boss, Apple Sauce"
– Andy Warhol

This book is all about turning your vision into reality, but before we can create our vision, we must understand our current reality. After all, current reality is all we will ever actually get to experience and our current reality has been shaped - moment by moment, decision by decision, day by day. I did not wake up this morning, roll out of bed and magically become Jeff Moore. Just as Tiger Woods didn't wake up and magically become Tiger Woods, nor did you wake up this morning and magically become you.

We all have continued to take action steps every day in building this person we now are - the process never ends.

> **"In the long run, we shape our own lives and we shape ourselves. The process never ends until we die. And the choices we make are ultimately our own responsibility."**
> **– *Eleanor Roosevelt***

If you are really serious about turning your vision into reality, then you must first become your own leader. The reason is simple. If you don't take charge of your life, someone else will. And the best way to take the leadership role of your life is to begin by controlling the meaning of your circumstances and adversities, rather than having them control you. Essentially, you see opportunity where others don't.

> **"Leadership is practiced not so much in words as in attitude and actions."**
> **– *Harold S. Geneen***

Self-Leadership

When I think of self-leadership I immediately think of Terry Fox, "Mr. Self-Leadership." Really stop and think about this for a second. Was Terry the first young male in the history of the world to lose his leg to cancer? The answer to that is, of course not. So why then do we know and celebrate Terry. The answer is clear - because Terry stepped up. He took the same adversity, the same challenge that many have faced before him and did something about it. Terry ran further on one leg than most will run in their entire lives (3,330 miles in just 143 days, to be exact, all while raising over 24 million dollars to help fight that which stole his leg). Terry is a classic example of what taking control and becoming your own leader is all about.

I know what you're thinking. "Great Jeff, Terry was outstanding and he did change the world, but what does that have to do with me?"

It's all about meaning

The difference between Terry and most of the world is Terry's ability to give a positive meaning to his adversity. Terry could have easily packed it up, sat on his couch and eaten Cheetos. He could have felt sorry for himself, but he didn't and the world is a better place because of that.

> **"Circumstances do not make the man – they reveal him."**
> **– *James Allen***

Terry exemplifies self-leadership by taking adversity and turning it into an opportunity. How can you do the same today? By understanding that it is not what happens to us in life but rather the meaning we give it.

The story of Hillary and Monica

Hillary and Monica are identical twins; their story begins with tragedy as unfortunately their mother passes away during labour. Hillary and Monica are raised by their father who handles their mother's death horribly - when he is not in jail, you can usually find him drunk and physically and emotionally abusing his two girls. Hillary and Monica's story is an interesting one because of the different paths they take. Hillary grows up the spitting image of her father; she becomes a stripper whom you can usually find in the drunk tank, Thursday to Sunday. While her sister Monica becomes a successful lawyer, a partner in her firm, and has the beautiful house and family to go with it. In fact, the twins are such opposites that a local news station actually does a story on them. One at a time, the interviewer sits down with each sister, and then asks her to talk about her life. Each of them tells a remarkably similar story; the difference however can be found in the reporter's closing question. The reporter first asks Hillary, "Hillary, how do you believe your life ended up this way?" Hillary's answer is "With a father like that growing up, what else would you expect?" The reporter then asks Monica, "Monica, how do you believe your life ended up this way?" Her answer: "With a father like that growing up, what else would you expect?"

The moral: some people in life will be abused, and they will take that abuse and for the rest of their lives be a victim; others will take the abuse and find an opportunity to help others. Some people will lose a family member to violence and, in turn, think that the world is inherently evil. They will turn their backs on their fellow man. Others will experience the same thing and turn it into an opportunity to create peace. It is never what happens to us, but rather the meaning that we give it, that will shape our lives. This is big-picture vs. little-picture thinking; empowering questions vs. disempowering questions.

Better than positive thinking

There is a lot to be said about the POWER OF POSITIVE THINKING, most of which is complete BS. I don't want to burst anyone's bubble here, but there is more to success and accomplishment than just thinking happy thoughts. Yet with that being said, the last thing I want to do is minimize the importance of remaining positive when times are rough. I don't believe in positive thinking. I believe in positive empowering questions.

I wish I could take credit for "empowering questions", but I can't. I learned them from someone I believe to be the greatest motivator of all time. His name is Anthony Robbins, and without question, Mr. Robbins has changed my life. What Anthony, or Tony for short, has taught me is that when I find myself in a downward, negative thinking spiral, I must recognize it and then ask a better question, essentially interrupting the pattern. All of our life's self-talk, or positive and negative thinking, comes from evaluations which are really questions trying to make a distinction about what a situation means.

"Want a better answer, ask a better question."
– *Anthony Robbins*

How asking a better question changed my life

After being fired from my most recent of jobs, I found myself sitting on a picnic bench outside of my now former employer's office. At this particular time in my life, I had just been suspended from college for academic probation, I was broke, insecure and fired from the only job I had ever been able to keep. On a scale of 1 to 10, I was coming in emotionally at about a minus 5. As I waited for a cab to come pick me up I was unable to think of anything but how big of a failure I was. Then Tony's voice literally played in the back of my head, interrupting my negative self-defeating thoughts. His voice challenged me to ask one simple question. "What is great about this moment?" Of course at first my brain came up with, "nothing, you loser." I kept searching and then it hit me - I now had time to write the book I was dreaming of. I could become a voice for so many people who felt just like I did. Since then my life has taken a complete 180, and I have turned my limiting questions into empowering ones. My new favourite goes like this…

"What have I learned?" This allows me to go back and look at all of my actions, evaluate what went wrong, and move on. I encourage you to incorporate some of the self-empowering questions listed below into your life.

Five great empowering questions

1. What's great about this moment?

2. What have I learned?

3. How can I improve next time?

4. What approach can I take next time?

5. What am I prepared to do next time, to improve my result?

Five negative self-deprecating questions

1. Why me?

2. Why am I not good enough?

3. Why do I always fail?

4. Why does everyone else have it better than me?

5. Why do I even try?

Notice that the empowering questions seem to challenge the situation, whereas the negative ones accept it.

> **"Leadership is the ability to accept responsibility for results."**
> **– Brian Tracy**

Which leads me directly to the compound interest of your life. As I already mentioned, you didn't wake up this morning and magically become you. For me it has taken 26 years, 67 days, 15 hours, 12 minutes and 7 seconds to get to this exact point. Every single action has taken me to this point. Every decision, every thought, every lesson, every adversity, every challenge - have all been dominoes I have knocked over in my life. I could have been a million different people by now, but rather I am the person I am today - no better, no worse. The same holds true for you. We are the residual cheque of our actions and decisions in life. Better yet, we are life's compound interest. If you want to know how successful you will be in the future, look at what actions you took today.

The greatest contributor to our compound interest? Habits. That's why I do sweat the small stuff! Because stuff starts small and then grows. Just look at you - at first you were a baby who couldn't walk or feed itself. A drunk starts with a single drink; a black belt starts with one move; small actions grow and create your life …things grow or die!!!

Here is a perfect example. Let's say I wake up this morning and decide to take a new action step. I decide to not brush my teeth. In fact, I go the whole day without brushing, and for the most part. get away with it. I'm sure some people make a comment behind my back about my breath, or maybe about the spinach now wedged between my two front teeth, but for the most part my new action has gone unpunished. And so I decide to reinforce this action and do it again and again. My once little action has compounded over time, just like an investment. Now compound that over a fifteen-year period. Where am I? I'll tell you where - sitting in my dentist's chair with some serious gingivitis. It all started with one action, which became a habit and grew.

> **"My Doctor said I would have less nose bleeds
> if I just kept my finger out of there."**
> – *Ralph Wiggum (think about it)*

I realize for some of you this may sound silly, but think about it. If you are overweight it's not because you ate a brownie once before you went to bed and now are being punished. Just as if you are in top physical condition, it isn't because you went to the gym once. WE ARE THE

COMPOUND INTEREST OF OUR CONTINUED
ACTIONS, KNOWN AS HABITS.

**"We are what we repeatedly do. Excellence
then is not an act, but a habit."**

– Aristotle

Conditioning and change

Good news! It only takes twenty-one days to break a
habit and start a new domino effect. Even better news
(because who wants bad news), it only takes another 21
to install and enforce a new one. This means that if you do
it properly you can eliminate a negative self-deprecating
habit and replace it with a positive one in only 42 days.
In 42 days you can create a compound interest so strong
it can change your life.

Here is where it gets tricky. Most people are so conditioned
for instant gratification that they never last 20, let alone
42 days. We're so used to drinking something that gives
us a buzz, smoking something that changes our thinking
or turning something on that distracts us from pain that
we never harness the power of continuous action - we
never build momentum. Instead we reinforce our current
momentum and stay in our same conditioned atmosphere
enjoying the same conditioned results.

When it comes to our social conditioning many of us are
like junkies; we get clean for a little while, start our new
compound interest and begin to see minor changes. Then
something happens, like a call from an ex you just got
over, a deadline at work that you forgot about or some

other mini-crisis and it all flies out the window. Before you know it you're right back in that same old same old routine, mad at yourself for failing and since you failed yet again you wonder, "Why bother?".

So, how do you escape? Good question. Sadly the answer for most is, you don't. That's because most never truly become their own leader. Becoming your own leader means examining what is going on, discovering the opportunity and facing it by taking positive actions that over time become reinforced and create momentum in your life. While that may sound difficult, you are already doing this every day. The difference is that most will look at the adversity, not the opportunity, give it a negative meaning and then take reinforced action steps towards avoiding it.

We believe our significant other is cheating, but ignore our gut and stay in the pain reinforcing hurt as love, and then wonder why we're so depressed. We ignore the pain of an unrewarding job, live in comfort and feel content wondering why we live for the half a bottle of wine after work.

Your life right now is the result of all of your reinforced actions created by the meaning you gave each circumstance. Essentially this all comes down to one thing, "a decision", which we will cover in the next chapter. For now, enjoy the mini-workshop below created to help produce leverage and meaning to create a new life.

"Awareness Precedes Change."
– Robin Sharma

Exercise for Chapter 1

Becoming your own leader

Get out your journal, and ask yourself this one question, "What did I learn today?" I suggest doing this at the end of the night - review and reflect on the day that has passed - you may be surprised about what you missed.

Chapter overview

1. Find the opportunity or adversity

2. Your continued actions shape your life

3. Ask positive growth questions

4. Tony Robbins is the man

5. 42 days will re-shape your life

Ten great Self-Leadership quotes

1. "Awareness precedes change." – _Robin Sharma_

2. "Want a better answer, ask a better question." – _Tony Robbins_

3. "He that would govern others, first should be master of himself." – _Phillip Messenger_

4. "In the long run, we shape our own lives and we shape ourselves. The process never ends until we

die. And the choices we make are ultimately our own responsibility." – *Eleanor Roosevelt*

5. "My Doctor said I would have less nose bleeds if I just kept my finger out of there." – *Ralph Wiggum* (think about it)

6. "We must become the change we want to see." – *Gandhi*

7. "Leadership is the ability to accept responsibility for results." – *Brian Tracy*

8. "Leadership is practiced not so much in words as in attitude and actions." – *Harold S. Geneen*

9. "We are who we choose to be." – *The Green Goblin*

10. "Average people look for ways of getting away with it; successful people look for ways of getting on with it." – *Jim Rohn*

CHAPTER 2

I Am a Vision and Decision Away From Whatever I Want

"If you don't make a decision about how you're going to live, then you have already made a decision, haven't you?"
– Tony Robbins

If there is one thing I have learned about life, it is that we forge our path in life by the decisions we make.

You want to know why diets have such a low success rate? It is because the person on the diet never actually decides to change - instead they "try". The unsuccessful dieter may try to diet, but trying is not a decision. For them to be successful, they must alter their lifestyle permanently, not change it for 90 days. You can cut out carbohydrates for three months, but when those three months pass and you go back to your old lifestyle, you will experience the same old result (your residual cheque for compound interest). It is like an alcoholic going to rehab for 90 days, checking out and then going out to the bar to celebrate 90 clean. What's the point?

I believe that in life few people ever actually make decisions. I believe that most people think about things a lot, examine the ups and downs, but never actually decide. The way most people handle decisions is by procrastinating so long, that the decision usually ends up being made for them. The reason a decision can be so hard to make is because to make a decision, especially about change, you must have the belief that something is possible. This is why, to truly reach your full potential, you must first have a vision. A vision is really a belief that you can turn the intangible into the tangible. People like Walt Disney, and Jay-Z are great examples of what having and believing in a vision is all about.

The way to tell if you have made a decision and are not just thinking about something is easy - thinking involves nothing; deciding involves actions and results. There is no "TRY" in making a decision, there is only "DO". "Try" is like an apology to yourself or someone else. Whenever you hear the words "I will try to get this done", find someone else to do it. When someone says they will try, what they are really saying is, "Yah, if I get time I'll give it a shot. If not, I'm sorry dude, but hey, I tried."

In my first book, "Twenty Something in the Twenty Something's", I explained the math of decisions. Here it is again, in case you missed it.

The math of decisions

There is a math involved with making decisions; it is the math that creates not only the domino effect in our lives, but also the domino effect in our world. The math is very simple and easy to understand:

Decision = actions = results.

There can be no results in life without a decision. It is important to note that not making a decision is also actually making a decision. For instance, by not deciding what you want in life, you are actually deciding to take whatever you get. Every action has a result, and since that's what we're after, we must decide what result we want.

The job factor

Talent. We all have it, and yet few ever decide to use it. I am sure I will say this again in my book, but I believe talent is closely related with purpose. Unfortunately many of us don't have purpose because we have jobs. I understand the importance of having a job, but I would rather have a purpose - there is a huge difference. I do what I do because I love to entertain and help people see their own potential. I have found a way to create a nice income as well while doing it. If you're going to have a job then you might as well have one that creates a sense of purpose in your life. I believe you should decide to chase after a career that you will never retire from. For instance, a man who loves to create and work with wood should be a carpenter, because when he retires he will still love creating with wood. Our purpose is that which we could never imagine giving up.

Bobby boy

Bob is a skilled tradesman. He can create beauty in homes where there was once only rubble. He is not sure why but something about building sets his soul on fire with passion. Unfortunately Bob only gets to play with purpose and passion on weekends and sometimes after work. Bob's full-time job is as an insurance agent. Truth is, Bob does well as an insurance agent but his soul does not get set on fire with passion while dealing with the most recent of claims. Everyone who comes over to Bob's house cannot believe the beauty in the work - he has cupboards that pop with beauty, banisters that scream for attention. Bob's friends all regularly beg him to come over to remodel their houses. Unfortunately, he can't. Recently, Bob bought a new house, a new SUV and made other little expenditures on things that he really doesn't need. Bob's wife is consumed with "keeping up with the Joneses" and this forces Bob to stay at the insurance company, working overtime and hating his job even more. Bob now drinks three or four beers a night, trying to help quiet his boredom and rage. His underlying resentment of who he is causes him and his wife to fight every night. He is sick of having to watch the bills and worry about whether they can afford everything. He can't understand why he isn't happy; he has a beautiful wife, a stunning home and a great SUV.

He feels like he is living a dream, but whose? Every morning from Monday to Friday, Bob dreads going to work and doing the same monotonous thing and being unsatisfied.

> **"Most men would feel insulted if it were proposed to employ them in throwing stones over a wall, and then throwing them back again, merely that they might earn wages. But many are no more worthily employed now."**
>
> *– Henry David Thoreau*

The moral? What good is tangible success if your soul dies? What good is the house and car if there is no passion, no reason for living? The interesting thing about this story is, I believe, that if Bob and his wife (especially his wife) were not so concerned with "keeping up with the Joneses", they would be so much happier. If Bob and his wife had stayed in their small beautiful home, Bob could have spent more time working on his passion and maybe even turned it into his career. His friends were begging him to work on their homes - who knows, he may have made more money doing this. If this had happened, do you think Bob and his wife would fight so much? This story is open to interpretation, however I believe that if Bob and his wife both had focused more on fulfilling passion and not living large, they would be in a different place. (Ladies, this is not an attack on women enjoying tangible things, it's just a story.)

> **"Where the spirit does not work with the hand, there is no art."**
>
> *– Leonardo Da Vinci*

The I AM factor

The most empowering words in the English language are "**I AM**" because if you are, then you are, and if you're not, then you are not.

Before everything you do in life lies these three little letters: **I AM**. The question is, what are your "I AMs" standing in front of?

Above my bed in big black letters are the words I AM because I AM the sleep-in bandit. When my alarm goes off, I hit snooze and I begin to doze back off, however one of my eyes always peeps open and sees those three little letters, I AM. I realize that, yes I AM sleeping in and if anyone is competing for the same job as I AM, then I AM falling behind.

Creating a vision and making a decision to leave behind all that keeps you from your vision is exactly what a self-leader would do.

"What's crazy about standing toe to toe and saying I AM."

– Sylvester Stalone as Rocky Balboa

Exercises for Chapter 2

I AM a vision and decision away from whatever
I want

Exercise 1
Create

Without question, one of the most important points from this chapter is that you must have a vision for your life. Without it you are like a dog chasing its own tail or an explorer without an X on his map.

The first exercise is simple. Create your vision and create it without borders. Remember your vision is simply the belief you have about what you are capable of in your life. The question then becomes, "What do you believe?" - not what your parents have told you, not what your spouse has told you and not what your friends have told you. What do you believe? Get out a pen and paper and write it down; a full description of not only what it feels like, but what it is. Also write down how you will know when you have it. For example, "I will know I am financially free when I have two million in the bank." What is your vision? Go and create it!

Exercise 2
Write yourself

Describe to yourself where you are right now and how you feel about it. I discovered this exercise while journaling; I was asking myself, "Where am I today and what have I learned?" and was shocked to see what I wrote. I wrote to myself, "I am frustrated with my life. I try every day to become as successful as I can. I try to create my vision and yet I fail." What do you think I noticed when I read this back to myself? If you're paying attention, you should notice that word "try". I realized that as long as I was "trying", I was already planning to fail and telling myself, sorry. After reading this little paragraph I re-wrote it - with the words "I am working every day to become as successful as possible and while it is true I experience some set-backs, I am learning the lessons and paying the dues for my success. I am enjoying the path to my vision and will never give up." Do you see a difference?

Chapter overview

1. You Achieve what you Believe

2. Your Vision is what you believe you are capable of in life

3. There is no try, only do

4. Decisions involve divorcing yourself from everything other than your vision

5. I AM - because you are!

6. Creating a vision and making a decision to leave behind all that keeps you from your vision is exactly what a self-leader would do

7. Not having a vision for your life is like being an explorer without an X on your map

Ten great vision and decision-making quotes

1. "There are some people who live in a dream world, and there are some who face reality; and then there are those who turn one into the other." – *Douglas Everett*

2. "To accomplish great things, we must not only act, but also dream, not only plan but also believe." – *Anatole France*

3. "It's kind of fun to do the impossible." – *Walt Disney*

4. "As long as you're going to think anyway, you might as well think BIG!" – *Donald Trump*

5. "Cherish your vision and your dreams as they are the children of your soul; the blueprints of your ultimate achievements." – *Napoleon Hill*

6. "Sometimes things become possible if you want them bad enough." – *T.S. Elliot*

7. "We need men who can dream of things that never were." – *John F. Kennedy*

8. "Love not what you are but only what you may become." – *Miguel Cervantes*

9. "All your dreams come true, if we have the courage to pursue them." – *Walt Disney*

10. "Don't worry about people stealing your ideas. If your ideas are any good you'll ram them down people's throats." – *Howard Aiken*

CHAPTER 3

Killing Excuses

"Lack of action is the creator of excuses."
– *Jeff Moore*

Ohhh, how I loved excuses! Without question, I used them at every available opportunity. The problem was that I was the only person buying them. To say I had lost my integrity in certain circles would be an understatement.

I have come to understand that an excuse is a lie and nothing else. Which begged me to ask the question, "Why did I love lying so much?" The answer was clear - to try to protect my ass from the truth. I am sure by this point in your life you have discovered that yes, sometimes the truth does hurt. I know personally, I have on many occasions. What I have also discovered is that the most painful truth I believe I could experience is the "if only I" truth. The "If only I hadn't wasted so much time." The "If only I had really focused and gone after it." The "if only

I", hurt the most. I imagine myself being eighty, rocking in a chair, looking back at my life, wondering where it had gone. I imagine what I would feel like being haunted by those words "if only I."

"Fear not that thy life shall come to an end, but rather fear that it shall never have a beginning."
– John Henry Cardinal Newman

Excuses are dangerous because they temporarily let us off the hook; they allow us to not face the facts until it is far too late. It's the old "deal with it later" attitude that always costs us the most.

So what is your excuse? What do you use to deflect the truth and any pain that may come with it? How do you protect yourself from the truth?

I remember when I wanted to write my first book. I had one huge excuse that stood in my way. My excuse was that I could never write a book because I couldn't spell. Some of you may be saying "Jeff, that isn't an excuse ,that's the truth - you really couldn't spell." My response to that is "Nope. That was an excuse." Could I learn how to spell? Of course I could. It's one of those "If only I" that would have come back to haunt me when I was eighty.

As I have already mentioned, we tell ourselves and others excuses to protect ourselves from the truth of why we haven't done what we know we are capable of doing. We tell ourselves and others excuses to protect ourselves from the truth of why we have wasted so much ability and potential, and we tell ourselves and others excuses so that right now we don't have to look ourselves in the eye and say "I know I can, but I am choosing not to." (There is a decision and I AM.)

> **"The highest reward for a person's toil is not what they get for it, but what they become by it."**
>
> **– *Unknown***

Excuses are small-picture rewards, and if you ever want to reach your potential you must always look big-picture. The problem with big-picture is you cannot touch or see it right now. It's kind of like saving. You know you should save money, you know why you should save money, but that new watch would look mint on your wrist. Instead of saving you break and you give in … small-picture, and you get your small reward. Big-picture is you don't give in and you save. Fifteen years from now that money has grown by over 100 per cent and you're rich. The way to tell if you're doing big- or small-picture is to look at your results. Are you getting small immediate rewards or are you building and creating a stronger future? I am all for living in the now, but be smart about it.

How you have been trained for excuses and small-picture living

Usually when I do talks I focus on the emotion of boredom. I ask everyone if they are familiar with this feeling. Of course everybody puts up his or her hand. I then ask if anyone has ever taught them what boredom is and of course this time no hands go up. What I believe boredom is, is your subconscious or higher self - call it God, call it your spirit or soul, whatever. I believe boredom is one of these things trying to connect with you and tell you "Get up off your ass and do something!" The feeling of boredom comes with the feeling of guilt; this is because you know you are letting yourself down. What most people do to escape this feeling of guilt and boredom is to think small-picture. They change the channel, surf the net, light up something or pick up a bottle - essentially drowning the voice with anything rather than doing what the voice wants. Usually the voice is quieted by these actions, for the time being, and you have succeeded in your small-picture actions.

The problem is all of this adds up (compound interest), and though you may not notice it at first, it begins to take over. Now instead of smoking one cigarette (or joint - you know who you are), maybe you will smoke two because one just doesn't do it any more or, maybe instead of drinking one glass of wine you will have half a bottle, because really it's just a glass and a bit more. These exploitations of small indulgences begin to control our life and dig us further and further into the hole of comfort, created by small-picture thinking and instant gratification to cover our self-guilt and boredom. **LACK OF GROWTH IN A LIFE CAN ONLY CAUSE AN EXISTENCE AND EXPERIENCE OF BOREDOM; THAT WHICH DOES NOT GROW DIES.**

As we overindulge in our instant gratification anti-boredom ways, we begin to lose touch with reality and live only for the bottle after work, or the shows we can't miss. We live in denial. Our comfort takes over until one day we wake up and say "If only I."

So how do we escape this? Well it's really simple. First we take responsibility for our lives, admitting that we gave important meaning to our instant gratification ways, and we acknowledge that we created the compound interest that has shaped our lives up until this very point. Then we create a new vision for our life. We do this by creating a belief that "I am great and I can achieve as long as I believe." We then make a decision to begin moving towards our vision by recognizing the past and the way we allowed excuses and small-picture thinking to shape our lives. We then kill these excuses through action.

Action - the kryptonite to excuses

How do you kill excuses? By taking action against them! When I caught myself using the excuse for why I couldn't write my book, I challenged it and made a decision that I would learn. I went back to school, signed up for an English course and continued my journey towards my vision. Was it easy? Of course not. Did I become a great speller? Honestly, no! Yet every day I continue to work on IT, getting better and better, creating a compound interest. Now I have two books published. That's more than most outstanding spellers will ever write.

My analogy for excuses and comfort is pretty simple. Excuses and comforts are like being in an outdoor hot tub in the middle of winter. Yah, it's nice and yah, it's comfortable, but you know sooner or later you're going to have to get out. So what is the first thing you want to do when you stand up out of a hot tub in the middle of winter? Jump back in, of course. And while it does temporarily make you comfortable again you know you're only fooling yourself.

In my opinion there are two types of people in the world - those who live through excuses and those who live through action. The difference here is like night and day. The person who lives through excuses, when his time is called, will have plenty of daydreams, whereas the person who lives through action will have created his dreams.

It is not a game

As I mentioned in my last book "Twenty Something in the Twenty Something's", one of the most reckless ways you can describe life is to call it a game; the reason being that when a game is over, you can choose to play again - when life is over, it's over, baby.

So you decide - comfort and excuses or your vision and a life.

Actions always speak louder than words

Actions always do speak louder than words, especially in today's society where words seem to be completely meaningless. I find that I meet a lot of people who love to talk about what they're going to do but never act on it. To truly be accomplishing your vision you must be dedicated. This doesn't mean just saying the word; it means constant and persistent action. If I say I have a vision for my company and books and show this dedication by sitting on the couch watching Seinfeld and Laguna Beach reruns, then I have shown my dedication to be nothing more than meaningless words. As I have already said, true dedication means constant and persistent action.

One day of action is great, two is even better, 13 is outstanding and 25 is a complete waste of your time if on day 26 you decide to quit. True dedication means having your vision or goal and not letting anything stand in your way.

> **"I didn't get where I am by thinking about it or dreaming it. I got there by doing it."**
> **– _Estee Lauder_**

I believe that deep down inside of us there is more potential and ability than we have ever imagined. I believe that this potential and ability becomes a fire inside of us that burns with passion. It becomes something worth living for and creating.

Most passion starts as a small match and as we move forward and take action the fire grows and fuels us with new energy, energy that we never knew we had. When we live through excuses and small-picture instant gratification, we allow the fire to shrink or die. When you look at men like Nelson Mandela and the Dalai Lama, you see an aura or glow to them. I believe it is because their fire burns so strong for their vision that they can't help but glow.

Exercises for Chapter 3

Killing excuses

Exercise 1

Let's take a little time and do some reflecting, shall we …
lol. Seriously though, what I encourage you to do right
now is to identify some excuse in your life that you have
used to comfort yourself from the truth. This could be
any type of excuse, like "It's normal for my boy/girlfriend
to have strange people call in the middle of night that he/
she swears they don't know." (I am writing a relationship
book next, can you tell?) Or something as common as "I
don't have enough time." Remember, we all get the same
amount of hours; it's just what we do with them that
counts. There is an old saying that goes "What you do
from 9 to 5 pays your bills. What you do between 7 and
10 creates your legacy."

Exercise 2

Real simple here, kids (I do realize some of you are much
older than I am). What action steps could I take to kill
these excuses?

Exercise 3

When do I feel bored and how do I handle it?

Exercise 4

What else could I be doing instead?

Chapter overview

1. Excuses are self-lies to protect us from the truth

2. Boredom and self-guilt are caused by knowing you can do more with your life

3. Instant gratification distractions such as drinking, smoking, drugs, and television cause short-term pleasure and long-term pain

4. Actions kill excuses

5. Words mean nothing; actions always speak louder

6. Life is not a game

7. You fuel your own fire by the actions you take

8. There are two types of people - those who live their dreams and those who only have daydreams

Ten great actions quotes

1. "I didn't get where I am by thinking about it or dreaming it. I got there by doing it." – *Estee Lauder*

2. "The only man who makes no mistakes is the man who never does anything." – *Eleanor Roosevelt*

3. "Nothing will work unless you do." – *John Wooden*

4. "The highest reward for a person's toil is not what they get for it, but for what they become by it." – *Unknown*

5. "Do not wait; the time will never be just right. Start where you stand, work with whatever tools you have at your command, and the better tools will be found as you go along." – *Napoleon Hill*

6. "I'm a great believer in luck and I find the harder I work the more I have of it." – *Thomas Jefferson*

7. "Success is almost totally dependent upon drive and persistence. The extra energy required to make another effort to try another approach is the secret to winning." – *Denis Waitley*

8. "There are those who do, and then there are those who watch television." – *Jeff Moore*

9. "Grand adventure awaits those willing to turn the corner." – *Chinese fortune cookie*

10. "Just do it." – *Nike*

Chapter 4

Failure, the Lesson You Need

"When one door closes, another opens; but we so often look so long and so regretfully upon the closed door, that we do not see the one which opens for us."

– Alexander Graham Bell

So here is the deal. If you do all the things we have talked about up until now, I can guarantee you will produce one result. The result ... FAILURE! That's right, you read that correctly - if you follow my advice you will fail. And that's the good news!!!

Unfortunately our society again has been taught and conditioned with the wrong meaning of failure. In high school maybe rather than learning the capital of India, we should have been taught that failure is important.

Because failure is the lesson you must learn to create success in life.

> **"Failure is only the opportunity to more intelligently begin."**
>
> *– Henry Ford*

Super Mario 1 teaching us life's lessons

During my presentations I love to introduce an analogy of failure that Super Mario 1 (the greatest Super Mario ever) has brought to my attention. I came across this analogy a few years ago while taking a break from writing my first book "Twenty Something in the Twenty Something's." I was just about to beat the game when it hit me. Life is like the last castle in Super Mario 1. You see, the last castle in Super Mario 1 is a maze, but not just any maze, it's a maze with punishment and time constraints. In the last castle, if you go down a wrong staircase, you go all the way back to the beginning. If you go down the wrong tube, you also go all the way back to the beginning. So where is the connection between the last castle in Super Mario 1 and life? It is really quite clear - in life sometimes we will fail, sometimes failure will knock us back, sometime it will knock us all the way to where we started from. If we pay attention and learn these lessons that failure teaches, we can move forward and be sure not to make the same mistake the next time.

> **"Insanity is doing the same thing over and over again and expecting a different result."**
>
> *– Definition of failure*

To paint this picture even clearer during my presentation, I have an audience member come up on the stage. I then ask them to imagine that collectively the two of us have set a goal, that goal being we are going to put a hole in one of the brick walls in the room. I then ask my volunteer to go to the other side of the room and on the count of three, they are to run as fast as they can head-first at the wall. (I don't actually make them - I have them imagine it.) The volunteer imagines going to the other side of the room, running fast and hard at this wall and then Boom, what happens? The audience usually laughs and says the volunteer would be hurt. I then say, okay so we failed and learned a lesson. I then say to the audience member, okay let's do it again. They laugh and then say "That's crazy." I respond "I know but we're doing it anyway." So we pretend that the volunteer goes all the way back to the other side of the room and again, count to three and again run head-first into the wall, BOOM. We receive the same result. I ask the audience if it is crazy to continue doing this. Of course the audience says YES. I then ask "What if we went down to the Home Depot and rented a jackhammer, might this create a different result?" Of course the audience agrees.

This seems perfectly normal to most people and yet some many people wake every day, drink the same coffee, shower at the same time, drive to the same job and wonder why they are continuing to live the same old boring life.

In life you will need to learn many lessons. Failure is the teacher and provides the opportunity to gain these lessons. We can't always be right, we won't always make the right moves, but we can always learn. Always remember that in life the only time failure truly becomes a failure is when it is followed with the words - "I quit", which really means "I choose not to learn the lesson and stop." Failure is the progression to success and nothing more.

I understand that sometimes failure can hurt, it can seem embarrassing, and make you feel like you're 3 feet tall. The difference between you and everyone else now is that when it comes to success, you are aware of what failure is and as Robin Sharma says, "Awareness precedes change" and now that you are aware you can stay open no matter how devastating the loss or embarrassing the defeat and learn the lesson.

> **"You may not realize it when it happens, but a kick in the teeth may be the best thing in the world for you."**
> **– *Walt Disney***

If you look at Walt, the man is a perfect example of someone who failed numerous times and yet never quit. Walt had countless movies fail, experienced countless mistakes, almost went bankrupt and lost everything, except one thing - his vision.

Nobody has ever done anything great without failing; the greatest people in the world have been ridiculed and laughed at. Stay with your vision and never allow an average person's comments to affect you, for an average person has no right to pass judgment on a great one.

To truly create a vision (especially a great one) you will be tested, count on it. You will be knocked down, you will be roughed up, you may lose all your money. I believe these are all tests, tests to see how badly you want it. Do you want it so bad that you're willing to go through the pain, so bad that you will invest all you have, so bad that you will stay open to learning? Only you can answer!

Bad mommy

I realize that, as someone who is currently not a parent, I really should not be giving out parenting advice. With that being said, I have seen too many parents screw up their kids by doing the same over-protection routine, that I must speak about it now.

Susan is a great mom; well at least she thinks she is. She loves her son with all of her heart and never wants him to ever experience pain. When her son Mitch got his first bike she bought him every kind of padding he needed so he never skinned his knee. In fact for Mitch's whole life, mom always went the extra mile to protect him, which seems great, except for one thing. The only lesson Mitch ever learned is mommy will save the day. Mitch is now 26 and still depends on mommy to save the day. What if Mitch gets fired from a job, no biggy - mommy pays the bills; Mitch crashes the car, no biggy - mommy co-signs a loan so he can get a new one; Mitch spends the loan on booze, drugs and video games, no biggy - mommy will sign another; Mitch can't wake up in the morning, no biggy - mommy will wake him up; Mitch can't survive on his own, no biggy - mommy will make dinner, wash the laundry, clean up his room or whatever else he needs. Susan thinks she is doing a fantastic job. Yet she can't figure out why Mitch is so depressed, why he is so unmotivated, why he lacks confidence. The answer - because Mitch has no clue how to survive and has not mentally grown since he was six.

The moral is I know that momma bird wants to shelter and feed her baby birds, but momma bird also knows that one day it will be time for the baby birds to spread their wings and fly from the nest. So even though it's painful for her to watch, she allows the baby birds to try to fly and she watches them fall, but most importantly she allows them to fail and learn on their own. When parents interfere too much with their child's life, it blocks the child from the most important lessons in life - the painful lessons caused by failure. Failure leads to experience and experience leads to growth. One of the most heart-touching and important scenes from a movie that I have ever seen, which totally depicts what I am talking about, comes from the movie "Ray". In the movie child Ray begins to lose his eyesight and runs in the house and falls. He begins to cry and beg for his mom to come save him. His mom fights the temptation to comfort Ray and instead forces him to pick himself back up and become acquainted with his surroundings even though he can't see them. She does this because she knows one day she will not be there and he must learn the lesson now.

Exercises for Chapter 4

Failure, the lesson you need

Exercise 1

As we have already discussed, failure is nothing more than a lesson being taught to us. Look back on your life and discover a lesson you learned through failure that has helped you to become more successful. To do this exercise properly, I encourage you to go back and revisit empowering questions and self-defeating questions.

Exercise 2

If insanity is doing the same thing over and over again and expecting a different result, then are you doing anything that makes you insane? Relationships, money habits ... what lesson are you refusing to learn? Remember life's compound interest rule.

Chapter overview

1. Failure is an opportunity to grow

2. Insanity is doing the same thing over and over again and expecting a different result

3. Most people view failure as the end of the road when really it's just a new bend

4. If we didn't need to learn these lessons we would already have the result we are looking for

10 great motivational quotes for failure

1. "You may not realize it when it happens, but a kick in the teeth may be the best thing in the world for you." – *Walt Disney*

2. "Courage is going from failure to failure without losing enthusiasm." – *Winston Churchill*

3. "No man ever achieved worthwhile success who did not at least at one time or another find himself with at least one foot hanging over the brink of failure." – *Napoleon Hill*

4. "Failure is success if you learn from it." – *Malcolm S. Forbes*

5. "This thing that we call failure is not the falling down, but the staying down." – *Mary Pickford*

6. "Failure is only the opportunity to more intelligently begin." – *Henry Ford*

7. "I would have never amounted to anything were it not for adversity. I was forced to come up the hard way." – *J.C. Penny*

8. "Opportunity ... often it comes in the form of misfortune or temporary defeat." – *Napoleon Hill*

9. "You always find failure on the way to success." – *Mickey Rooney*

10. "Most people have attained their greatest success just one step beyond their greatest failure." – _Napoleon Hill_

Bonus Exercise

Creating the map for your vision

Ladies and Gentlemen: we have now come to the part in the book that I like to call "creating the map for your vision", which really means laying down the footwork for your life. For this exercise I need you to get a piece of paper - notebook or printer size. This exercise is about creating clarity. I know some of you are probably saying "Why would I do this stupid exercise? I already know what I want." My first response is "Do you?" And then, "Suck it up, dude. If you can't do a little exercise for your vision, you will never do the major work you need to turn it into reality." So humour me and stick with it. I don't believe a vision is really a vision or an attainable goal until it is written down - unless you can see it, read it and hold it, it's nothing but a daydream.

Step 1

I need you to put on your thinking cap for a second and answer this question, "What does every treasure map have?" The answer of course is an X or a destination. This is your vision so now let's make your X on your vision map. At the very bottom, let's say the last quarter of your page, I want you to declare your vision (write it down). If you don't have one by now, I'd say there is no time like the present to get one. Write down what you want for your life. What is your primary goal, or if you could accomplish one goal in the next five years what would it be? Got it? Good, now write it down.

Step 2

You need your starting point, which is right now, today, this very moment, at this moment, so put your hand on your heart and at the top of your lungs declare, "I am responsible for my life" and "I am large and I am in charge" and then write down "I am responsible for my life." Essentially you are declaring on your treasure map that "Yes, this is my job and yes, I will get it done."

Step 3

Identify your pitfalls or excuses that stand in your way. Create a box below the "I am responsible for my life" declaration and label it "My excuses" and then inside of the box list off each and every excuse you can think of for not creating your vision. This is to create awareness, and what does Robin Sharma say about awareness? That's right, that it precedes change.

Step 4

Great ... now that you have identified your excuses, create another box below the excuses box and label it "My action box." What kills excuses? You got it again - action, so let's figure out what action you can take to kill your excuses. Also inside of this box list some important steps you can take today to get yourself one step closer to your vision or goal. Remember, a journey of a million miles begins with one single step.

Step 5

We're almost there. Below the action box I want you to make another declaration that you will stay open to the lessons in failure. So here we go again, top of your lungs, "I WILL STAY OPEN TO THE LESSONS IN FAILURE." Now write it down.

So what do you have here? Well you have a nice little map to help you get started. Let's review. You have a declaration that yes, this is your job, and you are identifying excuses that may stand in your way. Since you are a smart kitty, you have also decided to get a little kryptonite and kill those excuses, and not only have you done that but you have listed steps you can take, this very instant, to get yourself closer to the goal. Also, you realize that in life you will fail, but hey, that's all part of the journey and so you have decided to remind yourself that yes, I will learn the lesson in failure and I will create my vision. Good for you!!

No excuse - we hurt during the creation of this or any other vision map ... lol.

CHAPTER 5

Paying the Price

"Nothing will work unless you do."
– John Wooden

Alone I sat trying to figure out my new vision map, and as I slaved away trying to forge a path to fulfil my dreams, I had a sudden realization. Wouldn't life be great if it was more like a grocery store and less like McDonald's!!!

I know this may sound completely out of left field, so allow me to elaborate. When visiting a grocery store the world is your playground. You are able to walk up and down the rather large air-conditioned aisles, picking up fruit and checking the firmness, taking a look at the meat and checking the expiration date. You can fill your large shopping cart till it overflows. Then you take your cart to the cashier and pay for your purchases. So, you receive and then pay (stay with me - I am creating an analogy here).

At McDonald's you also have a wide selection of items to choose from, however the ability to mix and match is not quite as large and no one can really guarantee that the item you want will look like it does on the menu. The largest difference, however, is that at McDonald's, after you choose the item or items you want, you pay first and then receive.

Let's review. Grocery store - select, receive, then pay. McDonald's - select, pay, then receive (hopefully what you asked for).

So where is the parallel between life and McDonald's as opposed to the grocery store and life? It's really simple, and since I am writing a book, I will spell it out for you. In life you must first pay the price to receive the rewards. If you set a goal, or define a vision for your life, before you will ever experience it, you must first pay the price. Someone who is overweight would never be able to create a vision to become as chiselled as Arnold Schwarzenegger was back in the day, go to bed, wake up being ripped and then start going to the gym. The math doesn't work that way. To put it in the most basic form that I can - the cost is the continued action and dedication you must show to prove, not only to yourself but the Universe at large, that you truly want it.

I remember watching Steve Carell on "The View" after the release of "Evan Almighty." The ladies were calling Steve a so-called overnight success. His response was classic. "Yep fifteen years in the 'biz' and I'm an overnight success."

In my last book, I finished with what I call "the prove it challenge" shown below.

Prove it

You want to be successful? Prove it!
You want to be the best? Prove it!
You want to be respected? Prove it!

How badly do you truly want it? I have listened to many who said they wanted something badly, but when it came to action, they never even lifted a finger. You want it? Go out and get it. Show the world what you have to offer. Show the people who have said you could never do it just how wrong they are. Open the eyes of the world with your personal shine. Blind the naysayers and conquer everything that lies in the path of your dream. This is your life: Take control and live it to the fullest!

I still believe today that those words hold the same truths. If I was to define my title or job I would say it is to be an advocate of action. Not a coach, not an author or even a speaker. I am an advocate of action and all of my work is concentrated in one specific field. "To get you up off your ass and doing something with your life."

"It may take a few years to put your success on track but it takes your entire life to fail."

– *Jeff Olson*

Get 'er done

He wasn't the most talented of writers, and to be honest really couldn't spell, but he never quit. He would have people read and laugh at his work, but he never quit. He wrote on a laptop that would freeze and lose all the work he had just created, but he never quit. When his friends were out partying, he was writing. When he couldn't get a publishing deal, he published it himself. When people said no one would buy it, he didn't listen. When he appeared on "Breakfast Television" his book went from a few copies sold to jumping a million and a half spots on the amazon.ca best sellers list in 16 hours. (Yah, I am bigging myself up - but it's not arrogant if it's the truth.)

The point is that I sacrifice most of my time and resources to create my vision. I don't just hold my hand out and wish it would come. As I mentioned earlier, positive thinking is important - who doesn't love an optimistic person? But with that being said, I know far too many people who tell me that they're just sending the vibes out there and letting it come to them … lol. Dude, you want it, prove it.

Exercise for Chapter 5

Paying the price

When it comes to paying the price, the most basic way to get started is to identify who you are now, and who you would have to become to accomplish your goal.

The way I discovered this exercise was while staring at a piece of paper. In the very middle of the paper were the words, "write a self help book and get published". I remember staring at these words as if they were Mount Everest. I then really examined my goal. As I looked at the words I thought about who I would have to become to accomplish this goal. I began making a list of all the traits I would not only exhibit but truly live and die by. As I went over the list it began to grow. Here are some traits that came out.

1. someone who can spell

2. sober

3. dedicated

4. not me

5. a finisher

Before I knew it I had over 25 things listed. I then looked at every one and asked why? Looking at the five I have listed here, it was really clear. First, I would have to be able to formulate a sentence if I was ever going to write a book.

- spell check works but it does not perform miracles. (As anyone who owns an original copy of Twenty Something in the Twenty Something's knows, a few got through. Oh well, makes it authentic.) Second, I would have to become sober, because no one would ever take advice from a pothead drunk. Third, without dedication I would easily fall off track and lose my focus. Fourth, not me ... the reason for this is that if I was able to accomplish the goal by being the exact person I was at the moment I did this exercise, then I would have already completed it. Meaning that I would be looking back remembering what I did instead of envisioning what I had to do. Fifth, I had to become a finisher. At that particular point in my life, I had about 30 ideas and projects I either was starting or wanted to try. To accomplish greatness you must have a singular focus and, most importantly, you must finish what you start. I have worked with many people who, when I ask what they want to do with their life, end up listing off tons of ideas and they feel confused because every time they start, they decide something else would be better. Make a decision on your vision, create it and then start something new. It's like a tree trying to grow branches without first growing a solid trunk.

Take this time right now and identify a truly worthwhile goal, then figure out who you must become or the price you have to pay to get there.

Chapter overview

1. You must become whatever it is you want in life

2. Paying the price means taking action

3. You want to be successful? Prove it!

4. Life is like McDonald's, not a grocery store

10 great motivational quotes about
PAYING THE PRICE

1. "The difference between winners and losers is that winners are willing to do things losers aren't." – *Dr. Phil*

2. "Things may come to those who wait, but only the things left by others." – *Abraham Lincoln*

3. "The most practical, beautiful, workable philosophy in the world won't work - if you don't." – *Zig Ziglar*

4. "Nobody's a natural - you work hard to get good and then work hard to get better." – *Paul Coffey*

5. "Just do it." – *Nike*

6. "Do the thing and you will have the power." – *Ralph Waldo Emerson*

7. "And I'm far from a Harvard grad - I just had the balls to actually do it man." – *JayZ*

8. "You can't build a reputation on what you're going to do." – *Henry Ford*

9. "We are who we choose to be." – *The Green Goblin*

10. "In the long run, we shape our own lives and we shape ourselves. The process never ends until we die. And the choices we make are ultimately our own responsibility." – *Eleanor Roosevelt*

CHAPTER 6

Pain and Pleasure - It's All a Matter of Focus

"Pain is no evil, unless it conquers you."
– Charles Kingsley

She was crying and upset, trying to find the meaning in this most recent of altercations with her family. I'm sure the thought of running away was in her mind; sadly she realized she had nowhere else to go. And so she turns to a notebook, to express her thoughts and emotions. These words could easily become a song, novel or movie. This pain that she feels creates an instance of perfect self-expression and creativity. This pain is that which she needs to move on and become the person she was born to be … a shooting star.

"It's a rough road that leads to the heights of greatness."
– Lucius Annaeus Seneca

We have all heard the same old story, "what goes up must come down", or "I never knew what I had till it was gone". But why? My belief (and it is only my belief) is that while I'm sure we would all love to live a life without pain, it is needed and absolutely necessary to create the best possible you.

When I look back on my life and I examine where I am today as opposed to where I was less than four years ago, I am amazed at my own personal progress. I went from a college dropout who could barely read and definitely could not write, whose future at best would have been mundane, to a twice-published author, successful business owner and someone with an incredibly bright future who has truly found his passion.

So to what do I accredit my turnaround? Well believe it or not, the answer is pain.

"Pain is no evil, unless it conquers you."
– Charles Kingsley

If I could name one tool for success that I have used to reshape my life, without question it is the ability to turn pain into a motivator. Instead of fearing pain and running from it I absorb it, breathe it in and hold it, then realize that it is my decision: either stay in the pain and feel sorry for myself, or attack it. When I wanted to write my first book I told everybody that I was writing a book and that I already had a publishing deal. Was this true? Of course not, however I knew that by doing this I would have only one option: get it done, or feel the embarrassment of being called a liar.

When I feel lazy or unmotivated I imagine myself running into a stranger who has seen me speak before. I imagine them saying they really enjoyed my talk, and wondering why I am now pouring them coffee. I imagine what it would feel like to be eighty and have one burning feeling in my body, the feeling of 'I wish I would have'.

Without question it always feels better to win, and it always feels better to feel loved than not. We have all been there in the face of defeat, we have all been there when the one you love, no longer loves you.

What intensifies these emotions of pain is the inability to see the big picture, the inability to know that through this pain you shall become stronger. Through this pain you are becoming more resilient and yes, most importantly, you are growing. Just as in failure, you need to learn the lesson of pain, and not continue the cycle.

> **"Man is not fully conditioned and determined, but rather determines himself whether he gives into his conditions, or stands up to them."**
> – *Viktor E. Frankl*

Focused thoughts

All right here's the dilly ... by now you are more than aware that we are the result of our life's compound interest, which is a fancy way for saying that our habits control our lives. Habits for the most part are really controlled by what we associate pain and pleasure to; this is NLP 101, and really goes back to giving meaning to things in our lives.

Think about someone you know who is always negative. They could be on a beautiful beach in the Bahamas and still complain about something small and stupid. Has this person always been this way? Of course not, but somewhere along the way something happened that was negative and probably painful. Since that time they have conditioned themselves that pain sucks and they should always be on the lookout for experiencing pain, so instead of focusing on the good in life they focus on the bad as a means to protect themselves.

I realize some of you are saying, "That's a real light way of discussing a much larger problem." My response is this: you get in life what you focus on. And your focus is controlled by your thoughts. Studies have shown that you think about 50 thousand different things in a day and only 1 to 5 per cent of these things are new.

I believe that you will never create your vision or reach your highest potential by focusing on negativity. There is no way to allow yourself to be open in failure and learn the lesson by only looking at what went wrong and staying there.

> **"Thoughts are things; they have tremendous power. Thoughts of doubt and fear are pathways to failure. When you conquer negative attitudes of doubt and fear you conquer failure. Thoughts crystallize into habit and habit solidifies into circumstances."**
>
> **– Bryan Adams**

If you focus on loss you will only ever see loss. I also realize that some of you are saying, "But Jeff, my loss was real, my friend did die, my company did go under, dude I did lose, and I must be aware of this so it doesn't happen again." Right you are, but that does not mean you have to live there. It does not mean that you should become a negative old man who can't see the forest for the trees. I know people who have lost more than anyone should and through the loss have created amazing charities, helped others in the same situation and dealt with their pain by giving that which they wanted most: LOVE. Then there are those who have lost and shrivelled up. They are negative, unpleasant, and wonder why people don't enjoy their company. The difference is their focused thoughts and, here it comes again, the question they ask themselves about what this means.

You don't get motivated, you do motivated

So often I hear people say, "I wish I was more motivated" or "I wish I had the energy to do these things I need to do." Usually this comes from the person who just got up at noon and is now lying down on the couch watching TV. The reason you feel lazy is probably because you are thinking about how much work you have to do and associating some kind of pain to it.

The way we feel and hold our body is controlled by our focused thoughts. I have never heard a marathon runner say "I'm too tired to go for a walk." Think about it. If I wanted to put myself in a negative self-defeated state, how would I do it? Well, the first thing I would do is focus on sad, going-nowhere thoughts. I got it, I'm going to focus on the last scene of *The Notebook*. Okay they're crawling into bed, they love each other, it's the morning and they're dead … got it. Now I'm going to focus on a really painful failure. Okay even better, okay now I am dropping my shoulders, and breathing shallow. Dude I am there, I am depressed and you know what? I don't feel much like writing right now … Moore out.

Okay now let's say I want to get out of this state. What can I do? Well how about for starters I change the way I am standing; shoulders back, standing straight, feeling better. Okay how about some deep cleansing breaths. Ohhh I am there. Now how about some positive thinking? How about focusing on the release of this book? Yah, how about the feeling of rocking 800 students? Dude I got it. Yah, now I'm feeling better. I realize that may seem a bit absurd, but your emotional states are controlled by the way you physically hold yourself and the thoughts you focus on.

Whatever you focus on is what you will receive.

Exercise for Chapter 6

Pain and Pleasure - it's all a matter of focus

Exercise 1

Identify a few painful experiences from your past and identify why they were painful. Then ask yourself this question, "What is great about this?" I realize at first most people's response will be nothing. It sucked then and it actually hurts now thinking about it. STOP. Remember the difference between empowering questions and self-limiting questions. Think about what you learned from this. If you lost a loved one, maybe you learned that life is short and precious, so love all you can while you have this time. Maybe you think of a time when financially you were crushed; this may force you to get frustrated and upset. STOP. How did you, or are you, bouncing back and what did you learn about yourself? One of the great lessons I have learned in life, from great authors and motivators, like Tony Robbins, is that our life's meaning and answers are shaped by the questions we ask ourselves. So, what questions are you asking? Growth and empowering ones or negative self-depriving ones?

Chapter overview

1. Pain provides growth and helps us to become stronger

2. We can use pain as a motivator

3. We recycle our thoughts on a daily basis

4. We receive what we focus on

Ten great pain and thought quotes

1. "It's a rough road that leads to the heights of greatness." – *Lucius Annaeus Seneca*

2. "Nature has placed mankind under the government of two sovereign masters, pain and pleasure." – *Jeremy Bentham*

3. "Pain is the great teacher of mankind. Beneath its breath souls develop." – *Marie von Ebner Eschenbach*

4. "There has never been a great athlete who did not know what pain is." – *Bill Bradley*

5. "Pain is no evil, unless it conquers you." – *Charles Kingsley*

6. "All we are is the result of what we have thought of." – *Buddha*

7. "Thoughts are things; they have tremendous power. Thoughts of doubt and fear are pathways to failure. When you conquer negative attitudes of doubt and fear you conquer failure. Thoughts crystallize into habit and habit solidifies into circumstances." – *Bryan Adams*

8. "You cannot escape the results of your thoughts … Whatever your present environment may be, you will fall, remain or rise with your thoughts,

your vision, your ideal. You will become as small as your controlling desire, as great as your dominant aspiration." – *James Allen*

9. "How you think when you lose determines how long it will be until you win." – *Gilbert K. Chesterton*

10. "In the long run, we shape our own lives and we shape ourselves. The process never ends until we die. And the choices we make are ultimately our own responsibility." – *Eleanor Roosevelt*

CHAPTER 7

You Are the Vision

"You know who you are, don't let them hold you down, reach for the stars."
– *From Juicy by Notorious B.I.G.*

Maybe it's the second cup of fabulous Tim Horton's coffee, or maybe it's because I just watched "Evan Almighty" (that movie always chokes me up) or maybe it's both. But right now at this very moment things are very clear to me. I write this today not in a perfect world, but with a perfect understanding of my world. There are things right now that weigh on my heart, trusts that have broken and yet, as Biggie Smalls would say, "It's all good baby baby" especially after taking time to reflect on the following quote from Morgan Freeman who plays God in "Evan Almighty."

> **"Let me ask you something. If someone prays for patience, you think God gives them patience? Or does He give them the opportunity to be patient? If he prayed for courage, does God give him courage, or does He give him an opportunity to be courageous? If someone prayed for the family to be closer, do you think God zaps them with warm fuzzy feelings, or does He give them opportunities to love each other?"**
>
> *– Morgan Freeman as God in "Evan Almighty"*

This quote alone has reshaped my life and always brings a tear to my eye, because of the honesty and self-reflection it provides. If we dare to live our vision, if we dare to create our dreams and reach our potential, then we must be able to see the opportunities that we asked for, and learn the lesson we need. We must learn to let go and allow our own greatness to take over.

I know every day I am tested, I know every night I go to bed asking for an ability to reach a new level of success. I have come to realize that this doesn't always come in the form I want it to. Sometimes it comes in challenges I hate, sometimes it comes in painful break-ups and things I don't want to experience, and sometimes it's great.

My message for this chapter is simple - sometimes in life we get so wrapped up in losses and pain that we can't see the forest for the trees. As Viktor Frankl talks about in his life-changing book, "Man's Search For Meaning", "To invoke an analogy, consider a movie: it consists of thousands upon thousands of individual pictures, and each of them makes sense and carries a meaning, yet the meaning of the whole film cannot be seen before its last sequence is shown." This is a classic painting of big-picture vs. small-picture.

I know that every night I ask to become more successful; I ask to grow and gain experience in life to reach my fullest potential. I understand that what I am actually asking for is an opportunity; I understand that opportunity usually comes in the form of a test, whether it's an opportunity to work on my book and then the phone rings and it's a bunch of friends asking me to come out, or a relationship that fails and leaves me lost. These are opportunities to grow, learn, feel and experience. Do I always enjoy these opportunities? Of course not! Some of them hurt, and push me further than I am willing to go. Opportunity does not always come as you're walking down the street and someone decides you should be a model; opportunity usually comes when we say hi to all the possibilities and use large picture thinking.

Your opportunity right now

Here it is - another opportunity, another chance to grow. What you do with it will add to your compound interest and shape your life forever. This is an opportunity to allow - allow yourself to reconnect to passion. I know too many people who have amazing talents; talent is another word for things we should be doing with our lives. These people are artsy in many different ways; some can design and create, yet sit at a desk all day. Others can heal and help, yet never do. Why? The "why" is because they lost their inner voice, clouded with fear and expectations. They created excuses like, when the kids are older or when I have more money, and yet the time will never come. Inside, that voice would die to sing and be heard; that voice begs for your attention, so allow, reconnect.

Your purpose is connected with your passion, and usually passion creates talent. We fight ourselves the whole way, saying it's silly or not today, but if not today then when? When do we live, when do we excel, when do we become who we were born to be? If not in this moment, then when? You are all you need to be right now. The journey begins with who you are today and ends with who you were born to become, if you are willing to chase and allow. It's not easy - if it was everyone would do it. You will be ridiculed, crushed and challenged, just as you will feel joy and triumph. As a good friend of mine says, "Live, Love and Laugh."

How to begin

By now we have already covered many ways to get started. If you haven't started already then I suggest you go somewhere by yourself, pour yourself a coffee, tea, glass of wine, whatever. Relax, light a candle - heck, light a few - take some deep breaths and do not speak. For this moment only, block out everything else in your mind and focus only on the future. Visualize how you want it to be, then write it down and then allow yourself to connect with that feeling. Experience the joy it is to be you, then go out there and take one step, starting today, to get yourself there. Follow it with another and then another, take notes along the way, discover what does and doesn't work. Learn the lesson. Say hi to the possibilities and opportunities and create. Live Love and Laugh. You can become who you were meant to be, if you decide!

As Cesar Pareso put it so well, "We do not remember days; we remember moments." So go out and create a moment you will never forget.

My final words

Here is what I know after 26 years on this planet.

I know that things don't make sense sometimes but the more we try to fight change, the worse we make it on ourselves.

I know that a sweet lie is always easier to take than a painful truth, but always more dangerous as well. You must face your truths, even the ones you don't want.

I know to always trust my gut, because it is never wrong.

I know that we all make mistakes.

I know that you can't be what you can't believe.

I know that who I am today will shape who I become tomorrow.

And most importantly, I know the greatest piece of art you will ever create is the one you call your life, so go out there and use all the colours you can find - use the blues of sadness, the yellows of success and the greens of opportunity.

Exercise for Chapter 7

You are the vision

Question 1

We all have so much talent, so much ability, and so much potential. How are you using yours?

Exercise 1

Go out and become who you were meant to be!!!

Chapter overview

1. You can do it

2. You have all the ability

3. You have all the potential

4. You have all the talent

5. Your life is waiting for you

6. Opportunity does not always come in the way we want or expect, but it does come

Ten solid closing quotes

1. "Let me ask you something. If someone prays for patience, you think God gives them patience? Or does He give them the opportunity to be patient? If he prayed for courage, does God give him

courage, or does He give him an opportunity to be courageous? If someone prayed for the family to be closer, do you think God zaps them with warm fuzzy feelings, or does He give them opportunities to love each other?" – *Morgan Freeman as God in "Evan Almighty"*

2. "I think I can, I think I can." – *From "The Little Engine That Could"*

3. "You know who you are, don't let them hold you down, reach for the stars." – *From Juicy by Notorious B.I.G.*

4. "I am committed to living my life to the fullest, by not judging and dwelling on my past, but by living for a commitment to being the best I can be in the future." – *Me*

5. "Few is the number of those who think with their own minds and feel with their own hearts." – *Albert Einstein*

6. "This is the beginning of a new day. You have been given this day to use, as you will. You can waste it or use it for good. What you do today is important because you are exchanging a day of your life for it. When tomorrow comes, this day will be gone forever. In its place is something that you have left behind. Let it be something good." – *Unknown*

7. "Fear not that thy life shall come to an end, but rather fear that it shall never have a beginning."
    – *John Henry Cardinal Newman*

8. "Our deepest fear is not that we are inadequate. Our deepest fear is that we are powerful beyond measure. It is our light, not our darkness that frightens us.
    We ask ourselves, who am I to be brilliant, gorgeous, talented and fabulous?
    Actually, who are we not to be?
    You are a child of God.
    Your playing small doesn't serve the world.
    There's nothing enlightened about shrinking so that other people won't feel insecure around you.
    We are born to make manifest the glory of God that is within us.
    It's not just in some of us, it's in everyone.
    And as we let our light shine, we unconsciously give other people permission to do the same.
    As we are liberated from our own fears, our presence automatically liberates others."

    – Source: *"A Return to Love" by Marianne Williamson*

    (As quoted by Nelson Mandela in his inaugural speech, 1994)

9. "The only limitation of life is the limitation of your own thinking." – *James Ray*

10. "A man has to have goals - for a day, for a lifetime - and that was mine, to have people say, "There goes Ted Williams, the greatest hitter who ever lived." – *Ted Williams*

Printed in the United States
119529LV00001B/61-72/P